The Walking With God Series

Discovering the Church

Becoming Part of God's
New Community

Don Cousins & Judson Poling

ZondervanPublishingHouse
Grand Rapids, Michigan

A Division of HarperCollins*Publishers*

The Walking With God Series

Friendship With God:
Developing Intimacy With God

The Incomparable Jesus:
Experiencing the Power of Christ

"Follow Me!":
Walking With Jesus in Everyday Life

Discovering the Church:
Becoming Part of God's New Community

Building Your Church:
Using Your Gifts, Time, and Resources

Impacting Your World:
Becoming a Person of Influence

Published by Zondervan Publishing House, Grand Rapids, Michigan 49530
Produced by The Livingstone Corporation. James C. Galvin, J. Michael Kendrick, Daryl J. Lucas, and Darcy J. Kamps, project staff.

ISBN 0-310-59173-2

Cover design: Mark Veldheer
Interior design: Catherine Bergstrom

Printed in the United States of America
94 95 96 97 98 99 / DP / 9 8 7 6 5 4 3

Preface

The *Walking With God Series* was developed as the curriculum for small groups at Willow Creek Community Church in South Barrington, Illinois. This innovative church has grown to over 15,000 in less than two decades, and the material here flows out of the vision and values of this dynamic ministry. Groups using these studies have produced many of the leaders, both staff and volunteer, throughout the church.

Associate Pastor Don Cousins wrote the first draft of this material and used it with his own small group. After testing it there, he revised it and passed his notes to Judson Poling, Director of Curriculum Development, who edited and expanded the outlines. Several pilot groups helped shape the material as it was being written and revised. A team of leaders labored through a line-by-line revision of these study guides over a year's span of time. Finally, these revisions were put into this new, more usable format.

Any church or group can use these studies in a relational context to help raise up devoted disciples. Group members who finish all six books will lay a solid foundation for a lifelong walk with God.

Willow Creek Resources is a publishing partnership between Zondervan Publishing House and the Willow Creek Association. Willow Creek Resources will include drama sketches, small group curricula, training material, videos, and many other specialized ministry resources.

Willow Creek Association is an international network of churches ministering to the unchurched. Founded in 1992, the Willow Creek Association serves churches through conferences, seminars, regional roundtables, consulting, and ministry resource materials. The mission of the Association is to assist churches in reestablishing the priority and practice of reaching lost people for Christ through church ministries targeted to seekers.

For conference and seminar information please write to:

Willow Creek Association
P.O. Box 3188
Barrington, Illinois 60011-3188

Contents

Discovering the Church

Becoming Part of God's New Community

Introduction

Many of us have felt some measure of frustration with the church. At times we can't help feeling that the Spirit-driven, culturally relevant body of Christ has become a confused and frequently ineffective institution. The church has been attacked from the outside, and compromised on the inside, and in many places it is showing signs of wear. Those of us with the courage to be honest realize that we have even made the situation worse on occasion. It is true that there *are* churches that have been faithful witnesses for Christ. But too many others have been put to sleep.

It's one thing to declare, "Things are bad." It's another thing to say, "Here's the way out." Anybody can criticize. We must go further than diagnose—we must revive. Small group members not only need to discover the church, they need to discover their own place in it.

People must *come together* to become the church. But members who come together to give, and not just to take, are rare. Your small group is a perfect place to change this pattern. The first steps toward "contributing to the work" can happen there. Not only will you experience the joy of the church in action; you can feel the satisfaction of being players in God's great plan.

By committing to this study, you are opening yourself up to some profound changes. You will never be able to look at the church in the same way, nor will you see yourself as you have in the past. This reality is the wonder of the church, the blessing of using our gifts, the satisfaction of being a contributor—relationally, emotionally, financially. This realization is what it means to "discover" the church.

A New Community

Having just moved to a new city, Daryl and Ruth were anxious to find a new church. They had written a list of "musts" that their church had to have—dynamic preaching and teaching, excellent music, a top-notch educational program, and activities for their children. But actually finding a church that met all these qualifications was far more difficult than they imagined. Some churches they visited had great speakers but almost nothing for the youth. Others provided wonderful music in their worship services but had no commitment to evangelism or outreach.

Finally, after weeks of searching, Daryl and Ruth found what they were looking for. What ultimately tipped the scales for them was not what they originally expected. A sense of community existed between the members in this church that was infectious, and they realized this church was experiencing not only relevant teaching, but relevant living. This was a group they could worship with. These were people they could enjoy serving alongside of. This was a place they could invite unchurched friends without embarrassment. This was a community they could call home. They had found—and wanted to be part of—"the church."

Like Daryl and Ruth, we should keep in mind that the church ultimately is God's people—not a building, a pastor, or even the special programs that we commonly think of when we hear the word *church*. This study will show you how God intended the church to function.

Life in My Church

1. The two words or phrases that best describe my church experiences as I was growing up are _____ and _____.

2. The greatest positive contribution the church made to my life as I grew up was _____.

3. My church experience growing up was lacking in _____.

4. In recent years, the church has made a contribution to my life in the following two or three ways: _____.

5. If I could no longer be a part of a church body, I would really miss _____.

6. In recent years, two of the significant contributions I have made to the church are _____ and _____.

Life in the First Church

Read Acts 2:41-47 and answer the following questions:

Why did people respond in such great numbers to Peter's message? (2:41)

To what did these new converts devote themselves? (2:42)

What did their actions reveal about these new believers? (2:42)

What did the presence of miracles and signs indicate? (2:43)

Why did the believers have everything in common? (2:44)

Why did these Christians sell their possessions for the sake of those in need? (2:45)

What conclusion can we draw from their practice of meeting together? (2:46)

How did the Lord bless these believers' efforts? (2:47)

What needs do the first church's activities point out for today's Christians? (2:47)

BOTTOM LINE

Bible

Schedule three times this week to get alone with God. Make your "appointment" whenever it's best for undistracted time with him. Read and study Ephesians 1 each time, noting observations about the passage and applications to your personal life in two separate columns.

Day One: Choose a verse of adoration from Psalm 145 and meditate on its content. Write down two benefits you receive from meditating on this passage.

Day Two: Identify three sins that you committed this past week. Is there any action you need to take to make things right (other than claiming God's forgiveness)?

Day Three: Make out a list of those things that God loves. Then pray specifically that he will increase your love for those things you've noted.

Scripture Memory

As part of the curriculum, we've included memory verses with each study. If you desire to make this discipline part of your discipleship experience, begin by memorizing this verse:

And whatever you do, whether in word or deed, do it all in the name of the Lord Jesus, giving thanks to God the Father through him.   Colossians 3:17.

Next time we will look at why the modern church has often failed to make much of an impact on the world. To prepare, consider the following questions: What qualities did the church of Acts 2 and 4 possess? In what ways does the church today fail to resemble the New Testament church?

Straight Talk About the Church

Tired of having to pay for expensive tools every time you want to do home repairs and yardwork, you call your neighbors together and announce that you want to start a tool-lending cooperative. Like you, they have each have a few items that are necessary for handiwork. Together you have just about all the equipment you need to do most repairs and projects. Your neighbors enthusiastically agree to participate, and the venture gets started.

On the first weekend, a few neighbors take a generous share of your tools for things they need to do around the house. Although you wanted to fix a few things of your own, you have no choice but to wait until next weekend. When that time arrives, no one is ready to return your tools. Worse still, when you try to borrow from a few of your other neighbors, they tell you that you can't because they are going to use their tools soon. After weeks of not being able to borrow anything, and with your items still in everyone else's garage, you realize this arrangement is a colossal failure.

When it comes to serving their church, many Christians are like these inconsiderate neighbors. They are glad to take what they can out of a local body but are reluctant to contribute to its well-being. This study will help you understand three present-day obstacles that hinder the church's effectiveness.

Qualities of the Early Church

Read Acts 4:32-37. In what ways does the church today resemble the New Testament church?

In what ways does the church today fail to resemble the New Testament church?

Why do you think the church today falls short when measured up against the New Testament church?

Enemies of the Modern Church

1   Rugged Individualism

In what specific ways has the rugged individualism of our culture affected the way you regard your wealth and possessions?

Read Acts 4:32-37 again. How did these early Christians regard their wealth and possessions?

How has rugged individualism affected your participation in the church?

What are some simple things we can do to be less individualistic?

2   Ineffective Spiritual Leadership

Why is effective spiritual leadership important for every church?

Read Hebrews 13:17. How does this verse describe effective spiritual leadership?

In what ways could you help the leaders in your church be more effective in their service?

3   The Consumer Mentality

Why is the consumer mentality prevalent among so many Christians?

Read 2 Corinthians 8:1-7. How would you contrast this "grace of giving" with the attitude of many Christians in churches today?

How can you become less of a consumer and more of a giver?

Conclusion

What are some specific steps you can take so that you can become a more active participant in your church?

BOTTOM LINE

YOUR WALK WITH GOD

Bible

Read Ephesians 2 during your appointments with God this week. Note observations and make very specific, practical applications.

Prayer

Day One: Meditate on Psalm 37:1-11. List all the promises God gives to us in these verses.

Day Two: Make a list of all the things that come to mind for which you can thank God. One by one, bring them to him in prayer.

Day Three: What is one quality you see in the life of another believer that you would like to have in your own? Ask God to begin making that change in you this week.

Scripture Memory

Since you are eager to have spiritual gifts, try to excel in gifts that build up the church.
1 Corinthians 14:12

The Church — More than a Building

At the base of the human brain is a small organ called the pituitary gland. By appearances it wouldn't seem to be a big contributor to the overall function of the human body. But in recent times, scientists have discovered that this tiny gland is a vital regulator. It secretes necessary hormones that are transported to other organs. With the nervous system, it coordinates and integrates those mechanisms that help us adapt to changes in our environment. It can also "tell" other glands to produce greater quantities of hormones. It is very small, but the body could not function properly without it.

Christians sometimes don't understand the importance of their part in the body of Christ. They agree in principle that they should be serving others and participating in the life of the church, but their actions belie their commitment. Others feel that they do not have gifts of any importance or that God cannot use them. Such Christian not only miss out on the benefits of active service but also frustrate God's attempts to use them in a manner pleasing to him.

By looking at four New Testament passages during the next two studies, we will see how the early church was encouraged to serve one another. In this lesson we will study 1 Corinthians 12:1-30 and Ephesians 5:21-23. This study will show you how God wants you to function as a member of the body of Christ.

Body of Christ

Have one person read 1 Corinthians 12:1-30 aloud. What important truth should Christians keep in mind when they talk about their spiritual gifts? (12:4-6)

Why does God give gifts to his church? (12:7)

Why are individual believers like the parts of a body? (12:12)

How can we feel confident that God can use the gifts he has given us? (12:18-19)

What reassurance did Paul give to Christians who don't feel their roles and contributions are very important? (12:22-25)

Write a paraphrase of verse 26. When have you suffered because a part of the body of Christ was suffering?

Why are some gifts more desirable than others? (12:31)

Based on this chapter, what two or three applications can you make about your participation in the body of Christ?

Bride of Christ

Now turn to Ephesians 5:21-23. Why are we to submit to one another?

Why did Paul choose the illustration of marriage to describe Christ's relationship to the church?

In what ways are you contributing to a healthy marriage between Christ and his bride, the church?

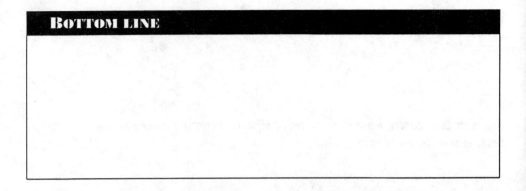

Bible

Read Ephesians 3:1-13, noting observations and applications.

Day One: Meditate on Psalm 8. Say a prayer of thanksgiving for the many ways God has shown his grace to you.

Day Two: Confess any sins that have troubled you more than usual in recent days. Thank God for allowing you to approach him in freedom and confidence (as noted in Ephesians 3:12).

Day Three: Pray for any three people in your group. Be specific in your requests on their behalf.

Scripture Memory

Now you are the body of Christ, and each one of you is a part of it.   1 Corinthians 12:27

Next time we will continue to explore the Christian's role in the church. If you want to prepare, read 1 Peter 2:1-12 and Ephesians 4:1-16.

4

The Church—
A Building of People

PURPOSE

A lone brick has virtually no value. Tossed by itself in the front yard, it is useless, even a nuisance. If it is placed in the street it will get run over and worn out. It may even do damage to whatever car or bike it encounters. But a brick properly positioned in a wall functions according to design and is supported and sustained by adjacent bricks. If each brick is placed with the others according to the architect's plans, it results in a useful and beautiful structure.

This analogy describes the role of Christians in the church. When they purposefully decide to go it alone, they are usually ineffective and can actually do harm to the body of Christ. When they are interacting with other believers, they help each other and fulfill God's purpose. This study will help you understand how the church is held together in Christ.

STUDY

Living Stones

Turn to 1 Peter 2:1-12. What are believers to rid themselves of? (2:1)

Why are Christians supposed to crave spiritual milk? (2:2)

Why did Peter compare Christ to a living Stone? (2:4,7-8)

What spiritual sacrifices are acceptable to God? (2:5)

What is significant about believers being built into a house? (2:5)

Why has God given such special status to his people? (2:9)

Why are we to live good lives among unbelievers? (2:12)

The Mortar—Unity in Christ

Now turn to Ephesians 4:1-16. What are the characteristics of Christians who are living lives pleasing to God? (4:2)

What is the key to maintaining unity in the Spirit? (4:3)

What two goals should all who are in the body strive for (4:11-13)?

What will unity in the body of Christ keep believers from? (4:14)

Why is Christ's lordship necessary to the growth of the body? (4:15-16)

What is your part of the work of the body? (4:16)

How does your spiritual condition affect the health of the rest of the body? (4:16)

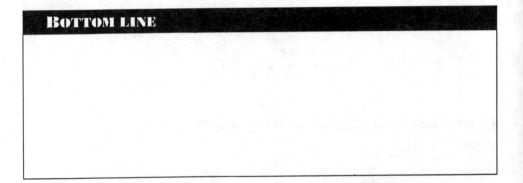

BOTTOM LINE

Bible

Read Ephesians 3:14-21, noting observations and applications.

Prayer

Day One: Use Paul's prayer in Ephesians 3:14-21 as a model for your own prayer for yourself.

Day Two: Identify three people for whom you can pray, using Paul's words in Ephesians 3:14-21 as a model.

Day Three: Pray specifically for each member of your family.

Scripture Memory

Review Colossians 3:17, 1 Corinthians 14:12, and 1 Corinthians 12:27.

Be Encouraged

Is there someone in your life you would call an encourager—someone who can give your spirit a lift with kind, supportive words? All of us can remember times in our lives when another person's words helped us through a trying situation or bolstered our self-worth—perhaps during the loss of a loved one, a difficult time at work or school, or even after a bad day. Encouragers also help us keep our perspective by reminding us of truths that we may have forgotten or ignored.

Such people are acutely needed in the church! The New Testament is filled with examples of believers who demonstrated an active caring for needy or discouraged brothers and sisters in the faith. In fact, different forms of the word *encourage* appear thirty-seven times in the New Testament. During this meeting, we will put the practical knowledge we have learned about the church to work in our group by doing an exercise that will help us build up one another.

Encouragement in the Early Church

Read Acts 18:27. How did the brothers assist Apollos in his effort to go to Achaia?

What resulted from Apollos' visit?

From this short passage, what general principle about encouragement might you draw?

An Exercise in Encouragement

1. Some positive character traits I've noticed about you are _____.

2. One incident I remember that made me appreciate you more was _____.

3. One quality about your character that I could use more of is _____.

4. Our group would be missing _____ if you weren't here.

BOTTOM LINE

YOUR WALK WITH GOD

Bible

Study Ephesians 4, making relevant observations and applications.

Day One: Pray that God will develop in you those qualities that will build up the church: humbleness, gentleness, patience, bearing with one another (Ephesians 4:2).

Day Two: Pray that the Holy Spirit will prepare and mature the people in your church for works of service (Ephesians 4:12).

Day Three: Examine yourself and confess any sins that have hindered the building up of other Christians (see Ephesians 4:29-32).

Scripture Memory

Be kind and compassionate to one another, forgiving each other, just as in Christ God forgave you.   Ephesians 4:32

Next time we will look at some practical ways we can make contributions to the body of Christ. To prepare, ask yourself: In what way do I contribute to the church? Am I a more of a giver or a taker? In what areas could I improve my service to other Christians?

6

Be an Encouragement

A high school baseball team is very enthusiastic about its chances for the city championship. They have good team defense, and their offense is a potent mix of power and speed. The pitching staff is as good as any around. But the team has a big problem. Its star shortstop is threatening to quit the team unless he can bat fourth in the lineup and pitch every third game. Angry and puzzled, the team holds a conference to decide what to do. The shortstop isn't a good enough hitter to hit cleanup. And he's more valuable as a shortstop than as a pitcher. The team desperately needs his contribution—but on the infield defense, not where he is so stubbornly demanding. After long but fruitless talks, the player quits the team. His choice becomes all the more painful when the team loses the semifinal round—all because of an error made by the replacement shortstop.

In the church, we all depend on one another. We all need to develop caring hearts and people-oriented outlooks that enable the church to work as a united team. This study will help you see the importance of making a contribution to the body of Christ through the relationships you have.

In what way is the church like an athletic team?

Read Philippians 2:1-2. What benefits do we receive from our union with Christ?

In what ways were these believers to be like-minded?

In what ways have you recently shown Christ's love to other members in your church?

How might you have allowed your own concerns to override your consideration for other believers?

In what specific ways can you make a contribution to the church?

Now read Philippians 2:3-4. Why did Paul caution these Christians not to do things out of "selfish ambition or vain conceit"?

Why is it necessary to consider others better than yourself?

Was there ever a time when someone practiced these principles to your benefit?

Who in your life could benefit from a more selfless attitude on your part?

Conclusion

What is the most significant insight you've gained during the study that will help you to contribute relationally?

BOTTOM LINE

Bible

Read Ephesians 5, making observations and applications.

Prayer

Day One: Go over your calendar for the upcoming week. Pray for each event, appointment, and so on, including family times.

Day Two: Choose a favorite worship song. Write out the lyrics on paper. Going line by line, use this as a guide for meditation.

Day Three: For what aspects of the Holy Spirit's presence in your life can you be thankful?

Scripture Memory

Do nothing out of selfish ambition or vain conceit, but in humility consider others better than yourselves.   Philippians 2:3

In the next study we will look in greater detail at how we can contribute to the church through our relationships. To prepare, meditate on Hebrews 10:24-25. Ask yourself: What motivates you to love God and others more?

The Power of Encouragement

Long ago, a country pastor paid a visit to a man in his congregation. This man attended church infrequently, always finding excuses for his lack of attendance. Upon entering this man's home, the pastor walked over to the fireplace, picked up the tongs, removed a coal from the fire, and placed it by itself on the hearth. The man thought his action very strange, but as they talked, the force of the pastor's illustration hit home. If you spread out the coals of a fire, the flame will soon go out. But coals burning brightly together can warm, comfort, and protect. We are "living coals," designed by God to burn brightest when brought together in close association. And in case you were wondering, the man agreed to attend church next Sunday.

This study is an in-depth look at Hebrews 10:24-25. The key question to be asked repeatedly throughout the study is: *What do we learn about being a contributor to the church through our relationships?* By examining these verses, you will gain an in-depth perspective on what fellowship in the church is all about.

After reading Hebrews 10:24-25, examine the following phrases from the passage:

And let us consider . . .

What did you "consider" this week–what did you mull over, plan, think about, and so on?

What did the act of serious consideration require in order to be effective–where were you, and what was going on around you?

. . . how to spur one another . . .

When has something spurred you on to action–what was your mental and emotional state?

. . . on toward love . . .

What inspires you or spurs you on to love God more?

What spurs you on to love others?

. . . and good deeds.

When has someone else stirred you to do good deeds?

Let us not give up meeting together . . .

What tempts you to skip out on times when Christians meet together?

. . . as some are in the habit of doing . . .

What could you do to challenge someone who didn't regard participation in church or small group as being very important?

. . . but let us encourage one another . . .

Why is encouraging one another sometimes a hard thing to do?

. . . and all the more as you see the Day approaching.

What is meant by "the Day"?

Conclusion

According to Hebrews 10:24-25, in what ways can we stir others to action?

Bible

Note observations and applications from Ephesians 6. Be prepared to share specific, personal applications at the next meeting.

Day One: Thank God that he has included you as a part of his church.

Day Two: Confess to God the times when you have hindered the work of your church.

Day Three: Pray for any corporate needs in your church that you are aware of.

Scripture Memory

Let us not give up meeting together, as some are in the habit of doing, but let us encourage one another, all the more as you see the Day approaching. Hebrews 10:25

In the next study the group will participate in another relational exercise. Prepare by thinking about character traits you would like to change about yourself or that you have struggled with lately.

Heart to Heart

PURPOSE

Many of our contacts with people on a daily basis are superficial ones. Given the pace of life, we tend to avoid sharing deeper concerns. Then too, many people don't really expect a truthful answer to pleasantries like "How are you?" In your small group, however, this sense of superficiality should gradually be replaced with a deeper sense of friendship. It is sad to have a small group that studies and prays together but doesn't build caring, genuine relationships.

This meeting will provide an opportunity for your group to share on a deeper level. Please note that the sharing shouldn't be forced. No one should feel compelled to talk about something he or she isn't ready to talk about. But we do encourage you to participate willingly, especially in light of the principles we'll be studying in this lesson. You don't often get the chance to share like this, so take advantage of it!

STUDY

Bearing Burdens

Read Galatians 6:2. What does it mean to carry another's burdens?

Read Romans 15:1-2. Why is it helpful to share struggles in your small group?

Turn to Colossians 3:12-17. What do you see in these verses that would build intimacy between people?

Sharing Heart to Heart

1. Putting all humility aside for the moment, I'd like to brag by telling you about _____.

2. Lately I'm preoccupied with thoughts about _____.

3. As I look closely at my life these days, I'm most concerned about _____.

4. If I could change one thing about my life, I'd change _____.

5. The sin in my life I find easy to rationalize away is _____.

6. I feel as though I have failed God and myself when _____ happens.

BOTTOM LINE

YOUR WALK WITH GOD

Bible

Read and study Romans 14:1-23, noting observations and applications.

Prayer

Day One: Pray for new Christians in your church.

Day Two: Pray specifically for your example around new Christians, that they may come to a fuller relationship with God because of your actions.

Day Three: Pray for specific guidance for serving Christ in a way that is pleasing to God and approved by men. (Romans 14:18)

Scripture Memory

Review Ephesians 4:32, Philippians 2:3, and Hebrews 10:25.

The Challenge of Following

To whom are you accountable? If you think about it, you are accountable to many people. If you are a student, you are accountable to the teacher to complete your work. If you are a taxpayer, you are accountable to the government to pay your taxes. If you are driving a car, you are accountable to law enforcement agencies to obey traffic laws. If you rent an apartment, you are accountable to the landlord to pay the rent on time. There are endless other examples that could be produced, but they all illustrate the same point: like it or not, everyone has obligations to others that must be fulfilled.

When it comes to accountability before other believers, many Christians become uncomfortable. Although they are willing to accept their fact that they must be held accountable before other people and institutions, they are reluctant to allow themselves to be responsible to and for other believers. They do not stop to think about how many struggles with sin could be overcome if they received the counsel and encouragement of other Christians.

This study will be the first of two on what it means to be accountable to God and spiritual leaders.

Accountability before God

What did Jesus mean when he said we are accountable for our words? (Matthew 12:35-37)

Why do you think our words are so important in God's eyes?

In what way is our judgment of others tied to our own accountability? (Romans 14:10-12)

Why is it important to make our lives count right now? (Hebrews 9:27)

How would you contrast accountability before God with standing before men? (1 Corinthians 4:1-5)

Why should we not judge anything "before the appointed time"? (1 Corinthians 4:5)

Read 1 Corinthians 3:10-15. What do these verses reveal about accountability to God?

What is the "wood, hay, straw" in your life? What is the "gold, silver, and precious stones"? (1 Corinthians 3:12)

Accountability to Spiritual Leaders

Read Hebrews 13:17. What does this verse tell us about how we should respond to spiritual leadership?

What responsibility do our church leaders have for us?

Look up 1 Corinthians 16:13-16 (especially verse 16). What qualifications do our spiritual leaders possess?

What does it mean in practical terms to submit to our leaders?

When is it right to refuse to submit to leaders?

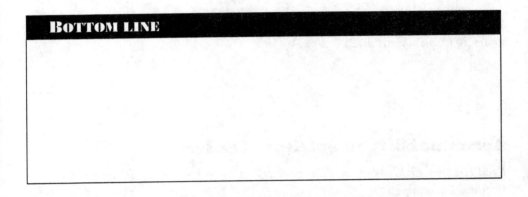

YOUR WALK WITH GOD

Bible

Read Philemon, noting observations and applications.

Prayer

Day One: Pray for reconciliation between Christians in your church.

Day Two: Pray that God would show you where you need to be more accountable to him.

Day Three: Ask God to help you in any area where you need to be more accountable to spiritual leaders.

Scripture Memory

This is love for God: to obey his commands. And his commands are not burdensome, for everyone born of God overcomes the world.   1 John 5:3-4

10

Am I My Brother's Keeper?

When Cain asked, "Am I my brother's keeper?" his hostility and defensiveness were clearly evident. In our day, most people feel the same discomfort in trying to establish close, intimate connections with other people. If independence and self-reliance are the heroic traits of our day, mutual self-disclosure and vulnerability are to be avoided. Even if we believe that there are advantages to nurturing in-depth relationships, we stay at arm's length because of fear and unfamiliarity.

This study will emphasize again the importance of accountability. It builds on the concepts on accountability to God and spiritual leaders by exploring our accountability to each other.

STUDY

What are the characteristics necessary for those who are "competent to instruct one another"? (Romans 15:14)

Read Galatians 5:25–6:2. What practical advice for being accountable to one another can you find in these verses?

Chuck Swindoll makes the following observation in his book *Living Above the Level of Mediocrity:*

"Accountability includes opening one's life to a few carefully selected, trusted, loyal confidants who speak the truth—who have the right to examine, to question, to approve, and to give counsel."

Next, we will look at four practical steps you can take to make yourself more accountable.

1   Open Up Your Life

What do you think opening your life would involve?

2   Choose Your Confidants

What strengths would a person need to possess before you would open up to him or her?

What would it take for you to establish a relationship like that?

3   Speak the Truth

What factors keep us from speaking the truth to each other?

4   Grant the Right to Examine

What does it mean to give someone the right to examine your life?

Practically speaking, how would you go about choosing a person who would keep you accountable?

What kinds of help could your accountability partner provide?

Conclusion

From this study, what would you say are the benefits of being held accountable?

What could you do this week to move in the direction of greater accountability?

Bible

Read 2 and 3 John, noting observations and applications.

Prayer

On each of three days, pray for one area where you need help with accountability *and* for someone else who needs such help.

Scripture Memory

Submit to one another out of reverence for Christ.   Ephesians 5:21

The next lesson is the third relational exercise in this study guide. Think about the following questions beforehand: What is a time when you observed something about another person but were too afraid to talk to that person about the issue—and it led to unnecessary pain for that person? What kept you from speaking up? How might the person have responded if you had talked to him or her?

11

Telling Each Other the Truth

Our modern society prominently displays a discouraging feature—lack of intimacy. Close, extended families seem to be a thing of the past. Even relatives who live close by too often do not show the kind of trust and authenticity we long for in personal relationships. The burdens of heavy work schedules, outside activities, tending to children, and keeping up with everyday chores often intrude on the intimacy between husbands and wives. Friendships, because they frequently develop casually and without real purpose, end up being superficial and noncommittal. We are a society of people all alone with each other.

One of the deplorable effects of this situation can be seen in how we try to talk to each other about what we see in each other. Our compliments often seem artificial and forced. If we try to offer helpful criticism, we tend toward opposite extremes: either we don't speak as honesty as we should ("polite people don't say such things") or we blast one another with expressions that relieve *our* pent-up feelings but do little to help the person we're talking to.

God never intended the church to be so out of touch with itself. Next to the Scriptures, his chief mouthpiece for messages of encouragement or correction is our fellow believers. We are to speak the truth to each other, and we are to receive the truth from each other. The church can't be the church without this interaction. This exercise may be more difficult for some people than others, but don't get discouraged if you feel a little threatened by the thought of deeper honesty (positive and negative) with your fellow spiritual pilgrims. But the goal of learning to tell the truth, and to receive the truth, is a goal for every disciple who wants to become like Jesus. This lesson will move you a step closer to that end.

How would you interpret the phrase that Ephesians 4:15-16 and 4:25 have in common?

Why is it so important for your spiritual well-being for the other people in your group to speak honestly with you?

What is the most difficult part of saying tough things to other people for you?

What makes it hard for you to say tender words to others?

Speaking the Truth in Love

Guidelines for Observations

The purpose of the rest of your group's time together is to give and receive personal feedback on each other. Observations can be either positive or negative. Your remarks should *always* stem from a desire to build up or help the person being observed. Positive comments should allow that person to recognize spiritual strengths that are a blessing to others. Praise should be sincere and not forced.

If you offer criticism, it should always be tempered by a concern for that person's well-being. Your observations are just that—observations, which are given from a limited but caring point of view. By saying "I observe," you are admitting you don't *know* for sure everything about a person's situation. You care enough to comment on what you see; be aware that there is always more to every person's life than what you perceive.

By proceeding with a humble, encouraging spirit, our truth-loving heavenly Father can use your time together to creating a powerful, life-changing event.

Making Observations

Here are some examples of how to state your observations:

- Mary [or Joe], I have observed that you _____.
- One thing that I really admire about you is _____.
- Dave [or Sue], I'm concerned that you _____.

BOTTOM LINE

Bible

Read the book of Jude, making relevant observations and applications.

Prayer

On each of three days, pray for a different member of your group who is struggling with a problem he or she brought up during the meeting.

Scripture Memory

Review 1 John 5:3-4 and Ephesians 5:21.

You have spent several weeks studying and thinking about the church and your participation in the body of Christ. For next week, think about five to ten ways in which you can apply what you have learned in your small group and at church.

Reviewing Discovering the Church

This study culminates your study of *Discovering the Church,* the fourth book in the *Walking With God Series.* Use this time to reflect on your experience and summarize what you've learned about the church. During the second half of the study, your group will spend extended time in prayer for the needs of your church.

Discoveries about the Church

During the past twelve weeks, what particularly striking discoveries have you made about yourself and your role in the church? Be specific.

Since this study began, how has your view of what an "ideal" church is supposed to be like changed?

In what ways can your own church be more like the church God wants?

In what ways can you contribute to the kind of change God wants to see in your church?

Prayer for the Church

Notes:

Bible

You are free to study any passage, chapter, or book of the Bible this week, but be prepared to discuss any observations or applications you noted.

Prayer

Pray for the needs in your church that you learned about during this session.

Scripture Memory

Review the following verses: Colossians 3:17; 1 Corinthians 14:12; 1 Corinthians 12:27; Ephesians 4:32; Philippians 2:3; Hebrews 10:25; 1 John 5:3-4; Ephesians 5:21.

Self-Evaluation

Your group leader will be meeting with you to discuss your current spiritual condition and your hopes for growing in your faith. Please take some time to reflect honestly on where you stand right now within these four basic categories of Christian growth. Rate yourself in each category.

+ Doing well. I'm pleased with my progress so far.

✓ On the right track, but I see definite areas for improvement.

− This is a struggle. I need some help.

A Disciple Is One Who . . .

Walks with God

To what extent is my Bible study and prayer time adequate for helping me walk with God?

Rating:

Comments:

Lives the Word

To what extent is my mind filled with scriptural truths so that my actions and reactions show I am being transformed?

Rating:

Comments:

Contributes to the work

To what extent am I actively participating in the church with my time, talents, and treasures?

Rating:

Comments:

Impacts the world

To what extent am I impacting my world with a Christian witness and influence?

Rating:

Comments:

Other issues I would like to discuss with my small group leader:

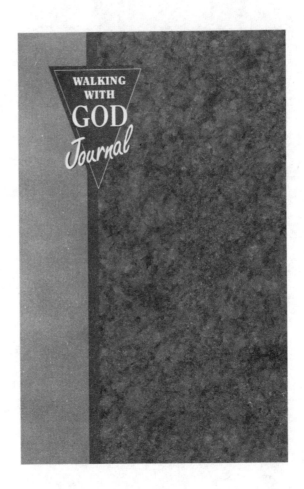

The *Walking With God Journal* is the perfect companion to the *Walking With God Series*. Use it to keep your notes during Bible study, record your prayers, or simply jot down your thoughts and insights. (0-310-91642-9)

NOTES

NOTES